Indoor Gardening

by J. Griffin-King

with illustrations by B. H. Robinson

Publishers : Wills & Hepworth Ltd Loughborough

First published 1969 © *Printed in England*

Introduction

Indoor gardening fascinates children as well as adults because it provides a great deal of pleasure in watching things grow.

Plants can brighten any room, and all that is needed for them to develop is sufficient light, air, and water. They do not like extremes in temperatures, draughts or fumes, and this is why bottle gardens are ideal for many plants. Bottle gardens can last for years without water, once the soil has been moistened and the bottle sealed with a cork or lid.

Plants in pots can make lovely presents, especially bulbs in bloom at Christmas, and tiny plant arrangements as Easter gifts.

Potting compost is recommended for growing cuttings and certain plants, but this is not absolutely essential if you cannot afford to buy ready-mixed compost. Most cuttings and plants will grow in ordinary garden soil. If you can find sand (which should be washed) and some peat (which is leaf mould found beneath trees) these will help some cuttings and plants to grow more surely.

Perhaps the most interesting things to grow are plants from pips. It is wonderful the way the shells burst open to reveal the first tiny leaves, and there are many experiments you will want to make.

7214 0232 1

Plants in bottles

You should easily be able to find some glass containers that are suitable for making bottle gardens: articles such as cracked decanters that are no use for anything else, unused goldfish bowls, sweet jars, goblets, and many other nicely shaped glass containers.

If you cannot find a suitable glass container, look in second-hand shops and antique shops for old glass receptacles, preferably with lids. Otherwise, if you do not mind a few hectic ventures to jumble sales, you are bound to find at one of these some suitable containers for flowers, plants and bottle gardens.

Ferns and mosses are ideal for growing in a bottle and so are many slow growing plants. The bottle gardens which have fitted or sealed tops will grow for a very long time without further watering, as they conserve their moisture. Another advantage of the bottle garden is that the plants last much longer because they are protected from dust, pests, draughts and fumes. Planted properly, with suitable plants, bottle gardens look very attractive and can become an unusual hobby.

The illustrations show some of the different types of containers which can be used. Small bottles should have only one plant which will not grow too rapidly.

IVY
and
SCALY
SPLEENWORT

SCARLET
PIMPERNEL

LADY FERN

AFRICAN
VIOLET

MOSS

CHLOROPHYTUM

PEPEROMIA

Plants in bottles—*continued*

Requirements for planting a bottle garden

Once you have obtained a suitable container, your needs for planting a successful bottle garden will be very few. You will require:

> *Some small pebbles for drainage.*
>
> *John Innes potting compost (obtainable from all gardening shops).*
>
> *One or two sticks for making holes for plants, and helping them into the bottle.*

If you have a very narrow-necked bottle, you may need a paper cone for inserting the compost and the plant. You may also need a piece of cork, pushed on the end of a stick or some wire, for firming the soil around the plants.

Preparing your bottle garden

First wash the small pebbles and drop them gently into the glass container which should be tilted so that the stones do not crack the glass. Drop in enough stones to cover the base of the container. Now make a paper cone and put it in the neck of the bottle. Pour in the potting compost to about one inch or one and a half inches, according to the size of the bottle. The paper cone prevents the sides of the bottle from becoming soiled, but it is possible to clean a bottle when watering its contents by pouring the water against the inside of the neck.

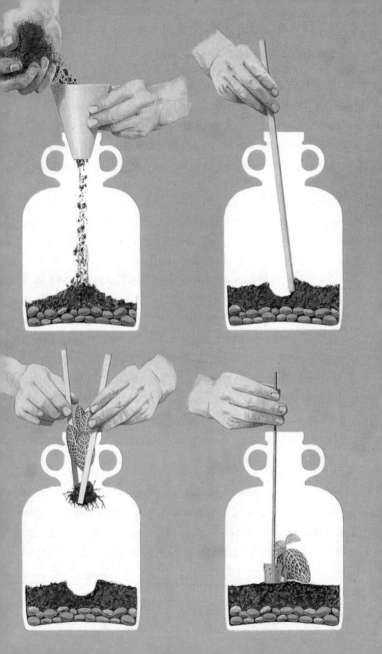

Plants in bottles—*continued*

With a stick, make a small hole in the compost and drop the plant in through the paper cone or with the help of two sticks. Straighten the plant with one or two sticks and gently firm the soil around the plant. Ease the soil over the roots so that they are completely covered.

Use only small plants such as a piece of rooted ivy, small ferns, Scarlet Pimpernel, mosses, miniature roses, sedum, which are among the wide variety available.

Some suitable plants for a larger bottle garden (which will need a little more soil) are: the African violet, which thrives in the humid conditions of a bottle garden; the Scaly Spleenwort fern (Ceterach officinarum) which grows three to four inches high and is illustrated opposite; the Athyrium filix-femina, sometimes called the Lady Fern, which is very pretty and grows in most parts of the country (also illustrated). Another fern which you can see opposite is Hart's Tongue (Scolopendrium vulgare).

When your bottle garden has been planted, moisten the soil and put the lid on. It should then last for several years without further watering or attention. However, if any dead leaves should appear, they should be removed carefully with two sticks, using them like tweezers.

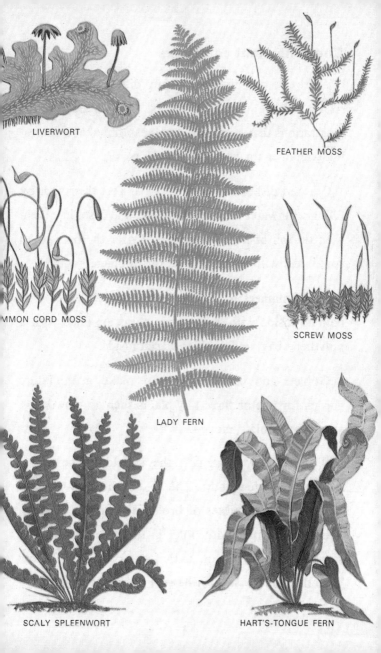

LIVERWORT

FEATHER MOSS

COMMON CORD MOSS

SCREW MOSS

LADY FERN

SCALY SPLEENWORT

HART'S-TONGUE FERN

Choosing plant containers

There are containers of many different shapes and sizes which are suitable for plants. You will see from the illustrations that even a little old teapot makes a charming container for ivy or other plants.

Cracked dishes may also be used. Test them first by filling with water to see if they leak, and if so, line them with tin foil or a polythene bag. Cover the base of all containers with small pebbles for drainage.

Tin containers may be used if they have first been painted inside with a non-toxic paint, or lined with a polythene bag, and pebbles placed inside.

Goblets and wine glasses can make a miniature garden for two or three tiny plants such as snowdrops, stonecrop, violets, etc.

If you use new flower pots, they should first be soaked in water for a few hours. The hole in the base needs to be covered with pieces of broken flower pot or small pebbles. The pots with holes in the base will have to stand in a saucer or pot, so that water will not leak out onto the window sill or wherever the pot is to stand.

IVY

CRASSULAS
PYRAMIDALIS

SPIDER PLANT

SNOWDROPS

CHRISTMAS
CACTUS

How to pot plants

You will want to know how to pot plants correctly if you are taking cuttings, if you are dividing a plant, if you are re-potting a plant which is growing too large for its pot, or if you are growing seeds, bulbs, etc.

First wash the pot, and cover the base with small pebbles. Spinkle a layer of moistened soil or peat on top of these, then put in the plant. Add more soil or potting compost, leaving half an inch at the top of the pot for watering.

Press the soil firmly, but gently, round the plant with the thumbs.

Pips, seeds, stones, etc., should be pushed only just under the top of the soil. A few drops of water should always be given to plants or pips when newly potted.

When moving a plant to a larger pot or miniature garden, hold the rim of the pot with your fingers over the soil and the stem between your fingers, and gently turn it upside down. Tap the base of the pot with the other hand, and the plant with the ball of soil should drop into the hand so that you are holding the top of the soil and not the plant. Then pot the plant, add more soil if needed, and water it.

Pips into plants

It is great fun to grow fruit pips, stones and seeds from trees, etc. An acorn will grow if balanced in the neck of a small bottle filled with water, so that the water touches the acorn. Transfer it to a pot of soil or peat (which is the leafy soil found beneath large trees) when the roots have grown well into the water.

Try growing chestnuts and sycamore keys, planting them in a pot of peat and watering once a week.

Unroasted peanuts in their shells will grow in a pot, and they are fascinating to watch. Gently crack the middle of the peanut case to help the nuts to shoot more quickly. Put two or three in the same pot, just covering them with soil. When the shoots appear within two or three weeks, you will see their tiny clover-shaped leaves.

Try to select fruit stones from fruit which is fully ripe, as these are the most likely to grow. You can even use the stones from fruit which is beginning to decay.

Label each pot with the name of the pips or stones which have been planted, and also write the date, so that you will know how long they take to germinate.

ACORN

SYCAMORE

CHESTNUT

PEANUTS

Pips into plants—*continued*

Many fruit stones (even peach and date) and pips will grow more quickly if they are soaked for two days in a cup of water. Hard shells should first be cracked gently so that the nut inside is not harmed. Plant in moist potting compost or soil in a polythene bag. Seal the bag by tying at the top, and put it in a warm place—such as an airing cupboard, or a sunny window.

Grapefruit, orange and lemon pips will begin to shoot within three weeks by this method. Then they can be brought into the light, keeping them in the polythene bag until the third leaf appears. Plant in pots and keep in a warm room.

Raspberries, strawberries, black, red and white currants and gooseberries can also be grown by gently washing the flesh from the pips in a cup of water, then drying on blotting paper before planting.

Grape pips will grow if pushed just below the surface of some moist potting compost or sandy soil.

Other pips which will grow after a few days soaking are apple, pear, cherry and many more including unroasted coffee beans.

You could grow all these pips and stones in jam jars or polythene bags, placing several of each type in each jar or bag. Some stones will take a long time to shoot, but others will grow very quickly.

ORANGE

STRAWBERRY

PEACH

DATE

Cuttings and herbs in bottles

Experimenting with taking and growing 'cuttings' of plants, which is called propagation, can be most rewarding and an exciting part of gardening.

A cutting is a small stem with foliage and a 'knuckle', broken from a main stem of a plant or tree. A cutting can also be one which has been cut below a joint (about half-way between two joints), with the lower leaves removed. You can see a cutting of a Geranium in the picture.

Some plants cannot be propagated by taking cuttings, but you will find it fun to experiment in this way: put about one and a half inches of sandy soil or John Innes potting compost in a jam-jar or preserving jar, and firm the soil around the cutting, giving it a few drops of water and then putting on the lid. Leave the jar on a window sill without any further watering, and within a few weeks white, hair-like roots may be seen in the bottom of the jar.

Yew-tree and other evergreen cuttings will grow in this way, providing they are not taller than the jar. Other cuttings which are too tall for a jar or bottle can be planted in pots, but should not be taller than nine inches. Leave the cuttings for as long as possible before transferring to a larger pot or miniature garden.

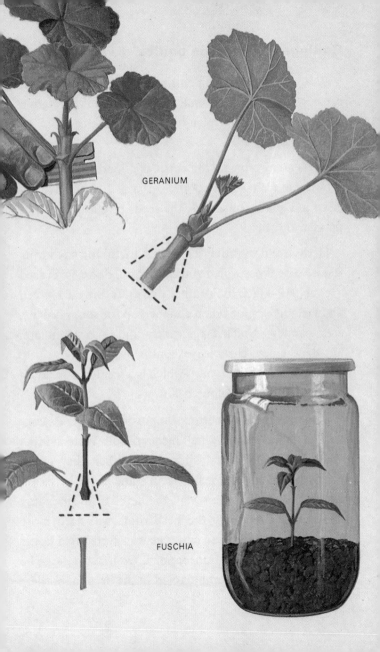

GERANIUM

FUSCHIA

It is well worth trying cuttings in bottles or jars, because roots grow more quickly, especially if planted in potting compost, and you can watch the growth of the roots.

You can also try taking cuttings of herbs, or you can grow them from seed in bottles or jars. If you have not any more glass containers, the seeds or cuttings can be planted in pots.

Herbs are decorative as well as useful for flavouring food. Some types which you can grow indoors from seed are: chives, which look rather like grass, are dark green and taste like onion when chopped up for soups, salads, etc.; parsley—which takes rather longer to germinate, has dark green, curly leaves and is usually chopped up for fish dishes; and thyme—which is a scented, spreading plant with purple-coloured flowers.

Plant the seeds or cuttings in pots of soil or jars containing about one and a half inches of soil. Water a little, and leave them on a window sill. When they grow, pieces can be cut off for flavouring, and as the herbs are cut and used this will prevent the herbs from spreading too much. Eventually the herb roots will need more room and the plants can either be transferred to a larger container or planted outside, or a fresh cutting can be taken from the herb and planted in the original bottle.

Parsley

Thyme

Leaves into plants

Growing plants from leaves is a simple and interesting hobby. The leaves of many indoor plants, such as African Violet, Gloxinia and Peperomia, will grow roots by a certain treatment, and so will those of some outside plants and shrubs. The best time is March-April or August-September.

All you need is a small coloured bottle such as an empty, brown pill bottle, so that very little light will enter. Now choose a leaf (not a fallen one) and break it off the stem so that you have the 'knuckle' and tiny stalk combined with the leaf.

Fill the bottle with water and cover it with a piece of foil or a milk bottle top, pressing the foil down over the edge of the bottle. Pierce a hole just large enough for the stem to go through, with the 'knuckle' in the water.

It may be several weeks before roots begin to appear, according to the type of leaf, but in the meantime you must top up the bottle with water, if necessary.

Allow the roots to grow to about half an inch in length, then plant in a pot and keep indoors. Continue to water a little once a week.

Experiment with different leaves to discover which will grow in this way, and soon you will find a leaf which will grow into a sturdy young plant. With African Violets, break off a leaf with at least one inch of stem and allow the end to dry off for two or three hours before placing in the water.

AFRICAN VIOLET

Foil cap made from a milk bottle top helps to support leaf and keep in moisture

BUSY LIZZIE

A curious show of flowers

Here is a way of growing flowers which will amaze your friends and which is fascinating to watch.

In the spring, cut a twig about one foot in length and half an inch in diameter, from an elder or any other tree producing pithy stems (a piece of bamboo is ideal). Split the stem from end to end and take out the pith.

Put the two sections on a sheet of paper, and place seeds of annuals (which you can buy in a packet from any gardening counter) at about one inch intervals along the length of one of the strips. You will also need a little loam or soil from the garden. This should be mixed with a few drops of water to make a paste, then spread this paste over each strip.

Place the two strips together, tie the two ends and also tie at intervals along the stick with cotton, but not too tightly.

Push one end of the twig into a pot of soil, and water the twig and the soil once a week.

In a few weeks, tiny plants will push their way out of the twig so that an unusual array of flowers will blossom from the same branch in the summer.

Plant arrangements

Hollowed out logs look very attractive when planted with a fern, Lily of the Valley or other plants, but if a small log cannot be found, plants can be artistically arranged in ordinary dishes or other containers.

The twig which you can see in the round bowl arrangement is set in a lump of plasticine or a potato in the bowl, concealed by pebbles or small rocks which also help to support the twig. Nearly fill the rest of the container with soil, put in one or two plants, then cover the soil with moss, shells, stones or sand if any of these are available.

You could make Christmas arrangements in this way too, putting a candle in a potato in the middle of a small arrangement, and making sure that the plants are not near the candle.

A tall plant arrangement with twigs could stand in a fireplace to brighten a room in the summer. Ferns and ivy are particularly suitable for this as they do not mind a position without much light. Plants do not like draughts, so if there is a draught from the chimney the opening should be covered with a square of cardboard.

LILY OF
THE VALLEY

HART'S
TONGUE
FERN

IVY

ALOE
VARIEGATA

MELANCHOE

Growing cacti and succulents

Most cacti and succulents are grown for their curious shapes and sometimes for the beautiful flowers which they can produce. Both originate from hot countries, so they like a warm room. They can survive without water far longer than most other plants.

Packets of mixed cacti seeds can be bought at gardening shops, and these should be planted in a sandy soil or John Innes potting compost, with a few tiny pebbles or gravel in the base of the pot for drainage.

If you have some shells or even large bottle tops which will stand up, then one seed can be placed in each, or if preferred, the seeds may be grown in a dish to make a cacti garden.

Sprinkle a few drops of water over the planted seeds, and leave in a warm, and preferably sunny room. Keep the soil damp, but do not water cacti too much.

Some cacti do not produce flowers, especially those which are not kept under ideal conditions, but there are cacti which will flower when they are quite small. Others will not flower until they have grown to a good size.

Varieties recommended for beginners are: Chamae-cereus silvestrii (red flowering and with peanut-shaped leaves), Mamillaria rhodantha (flowers well), Rebutia miniscula (scarlet flowering). The popular Christmas Cactus has bright pink flowers on the ends of its drooping branches. A fresh plant can be grown easily by planting a section in moist, sandy soil.

CHAMAECEREUS

HAWORTHIA

GYMNOCALYCIUM

OPUNTIA BERGERIANA
(Prickly pear)

FAUCARIA

ECHEVERIA

LOBIVIA

Climbing and trailing plants

Two of the most popular trailing plants are Ivy and Tradescantia. They look lovely trailing from a pot in a holder which is hanging on a wall or standing on a book shelf. There are many different types of ivy, and a pretty one is the variegated ivy which has green and white leaves. It will grow almost anywhere, even in a bathroom and can climb a small trellis.

Cuttings could be taken of the plain, wild ivy which grows out of doors. Tradescantia will grow almost anywhere indoors too, but the type which has leaves of green, pink, mauve and white needs the sun to keep its colours. It is the easiest plant of all to grow roots on cuttings. Just break off a piece at a joint and push it into soil. It can then produce three inches of roots within ten days.

Some other pretty climbing and trailing plants are: Saxifraga Sarmentosa—sometimes called Mother of Thousands or Strawberry Geranium; Climbing Nasturtiums; Passion Flower (Passiflora)—a climbing plant with blue and white flowers; trailing Asparagus plants, which will also grow in the shade. There are many more plants, but they might be expensive to buy or harder to find than the ones mentioned.

TRAILING
ASPARAGUS

SAXIFRAGA
SARMENTOSA

VARIEGATED IVY

WILD IVY

TRADESCANTIA

Trees in miniature

To obtain a small tree for dwarfing, you can either grow one from seed, such as those described in "Pips into Plants," page 16, or you could find a tree seedling a few inches high, growing beneath a fully grown tree.

Cut an orange or grapefruit in half, scoop out the fruit and, with a knitting needle, pierce holes in the peel all round from the inside of the peel. A cardboard ice-cream or cream carton could be used instead, making holes in it in the same way.

Almost fill the peel or carton with soil, put in the tree seedling when it is a few inches high, and give it a few drops of water. A seedling can take about twelve months before roots need trimming with scissors outside the peel to restrict the growth of the baby tree.

It is possible to dwarf fruit-bearing trees such as cherries, pears, oranges, apples and plums, which will all bear tiny fruit.

When the first roots have been trimmed, the tree can be shaped by pinching out lower stems or straggly branches. Stand the miniature tree in its peel in a pot with holes in the base, top up with soil and continue to trim the roots when they appear.

Growing bulbs

Bulbs can provide a lovely display of colour indoors during the winter and spring, and they are interesting to watch whilst growing.

Growing bulbs with pebbles and water

NARCISSI. One of the easiest of the Narcissi to grow is the Paperwhite, which flowers within five weeks of placing in pebbles and water. Fill a dish with small, well washed pebbles or gravel, one or two small pieces of charcoal (to keep the water fresh), and place one or two bulbs on top with the pointed ends upwards. Support the bulbs with a few small pebbles between, then add water so that it just touches the base of the bulbs. Place the bulbs in a warm room, and keep the water up to the base of the bulbs.

HYACINTHS AND OTHER SPECIES OF NARCISSI. These will grow in pebbles and water, if kept in a cool, dark place, from September onwards, until the leaves are three inches in height and the flower buds appear, when they can be brought into the light and warmth gradually.

CROCUSES may also be grown with pebbles and water. Put them in a cool, dark place indoors, and when the leaves are two inches high, remove them to a light spot, but do not bring them into a warm room until the flower buds appear.

Growing bulbs—*continued*

Growing Hyacinths in glasses

This way is perhaps the most interesting because you can watch through the glass, the growing bulb roots. If you do not have a special bulb jar which holds the bulb in the neck of the jar, you might be able to find a narrow vase (fig. 1), or use a drinking glass (fig. 2). For the latter, cut a circle of card a little wider than the jar, so that it rests on top. Cut a circular hole in the middle of the card so that it fits gently round the bulb and allows it to almost touch the water. Keep in a cool, dark place until the buds appear. As soon as they begin to open, you will be able to smell the beautiful scent.

If a bulb appears to be going mouldy, it could mean that the place where it is kept is too damp or has no air, and the bulb should be transferred to a more suitable place. The mouldy skin can be carefully removed and the original water replaced with clean water. The bulb should then continue to grow healthily.

Bulbs in fibre or soil

Hyacinths, daffodils, crocuses, snowdrops and some other bulbs can be grown in bulb fibre in pots, planting them in a deep bowl (to allow for root growth), on a layer of damp fibre and so that they do not touch one another or the sides of the bowl, and with the top of the bulb level with the top of the bowl. Add more fibre and press gently round them. Crocuses should have their tips just below the top of the fibre. If ordinary soil is used there must be some drainage holes in the pot. Keep in a cool, dark place until the leaves are three inches tall—one inch for snowdrops.

When the bulbs have finished flowering and the leaves have completely died, they can be cut off an inch above the bulbs. The roots should also be cut off, and the bulbs are then ready to store away in a dry, dark place indoors.

Some other bulbs which you can grow in soil or fibre are: Bluebells, Muscari (Grape Hyacinths), which are like miniature hyacinths, their colour is either blue or white; Sparaxis, which has flowers of many different colours growing to a height of one foot. Plant these from one to two inches deep from September onwards, and put in a cool place.

Do not plant different varieties in the same bowl, as some may bloom and fade before others.

BLUEBELL GRAPE HYACINTH SPARAXIS TRITELEIA

Flowering plants

Many indoor plants are grown for their pretty foliage, but it is interesting to grow a few flowering plants too.

Begonias are popular because some of them have large, brightly-coloured blooms which last for a very long time. You can try taking leaf cuttings from these. A Begonia is shown opposite at the bottom of the picture.

The plant on the right is a Geranium which will continue to flower from the spring, right through to the autumn or winter. You can see how to take cuttings from this plant in 'Cuttings in Bottles'—page 20.

The plant on the left is a Fuschia, and cuttings can be taken by breaking off a tiny branch with a 'knuckle' attached, and planting in potting compost or soil and sand.

There are many other indoor flowering plants, most of which you can grow easily from seed.

When a flower has almost died, pinch it out to give strength to the other flowers on the plant. If you want a few large flowers, instead of several small ones, you can pinch out a few buds to give strength to the remaining flowers on the plant.

FUSCHIA

GERANIUM

BEGONIA

Indoor water gardening

If you can find a suitable dish or glass bowl for a tiny water garden, then you will be fascinated by the little water plants which you will be able to grow in it. Such plants are sold in most pet shops.

Aquatics are plants which float on the water with the roots hanging down. One of these is Azolla Caroliniana. Another aquatic is the 'Frogbit' which looks like a miniature Water Lily. It has three white flower petals in summer, and in late autumn the leaves die off, leaving a bulbil which sinks into the mud until the spring.

Non-aquatics need to be planted in half an inch of sand or soil, with a few pebbles in the bottom of the bowl. Glass bowls are best, especially goldfish bowls because you can see the water plants and their roots from outside. Whatever type of bowl you use, it will need topping up with water occasionally.

Another kind of water garden you could make is one which is set in a fairly shallow, small bowl and placed inside another larger, shallow bowl. The larger bowl can then be planted with moss, stones and tiny plants, to make it look like a miniature garden with a pond.

Collecting seeds from plants

You will be surprised at the variety of seeds which can be collected from plants, shrubs and trees. They can be found in the most peculiar places—for instance, fern seeds or, more correctly — spores, are produced on the back of the fronds or fern leaves. The spores look like tiny specks of brown dust and are ready for planting when they drop easily by touching the fronds. You must cut pieces of the fronds with the spores attached, and place them in pots of seed-sowing compost or fine, moistened, sandy soil. Put small pebbles in the base of the pots for drainage, and stand the pots in an inch of water until the spores germinate. Keep in a warm room.

Many plants, including shrubs and trees, grow their seeds in the form of berries, but they can take many months to germinate if you wish to grow them. Look for berries which are fully ripe (when they are soft and almost ready to drop off the stem). Put the berries into sandy soil or potting compost, and water them occasionally.

Seeds can be collected from flowers as soon as the flower heads have died. If you wish to save them for planting later, make sure they are quite dry and place them in a labelled envelope.

NEVER PUT SEEDS OR BERRIES IN YOUR MOUTH. THEY MAY BE POISONOUS.

FERN

ELDER

HAWTHORN

HOLLY

PRIVET

HONEYSUCKLE

YEW

BEGONIA

BLUEBELL

POPPY

STOCK

VIOLET

Growing seeds without soil

It is fascinating to grow seeds on moist blotting paper or cotton wool, and many seeds will germinate in this way. Some seeds prefer the light and some prefer the dark in which to germinate, but you could experiment to see which your particular seeds prefer.

You will need a very clean container, preferably a glass dish with a lid, or you could use a jam jar. The lid is needed to retain the moisture so that you will not need to water the seeds at all while they are in the dish or jar.

Use clean cotton wool, enough to cover the base of the container, or a clean sheet of blotting paper, and place it in the container. Sprinkle water over the cotton wool or blotting paper until it has absorbed all the water it can without any surplus. Sprinkle the seeds over this and seal the container.

Keep the seeds in a warm room, and when they begin to shoot, carefully lift the seedlings out one by one and plant them in potting compost or soil, about one inch apart, using a jar or open dishes if they are to be kept in a warm room.

When the seedlings have grown a little more, they can be transferred to individual pots.

Watering and caring for plants

Plants need a little more water during the summer than in winter, and it should be given before the soil becomes dry. Over-watering can kill a plant, but most plants like a few drops of tepid water twice a week in summer, and once a week in winter, except bottle gardens which hardly ever need watering.

Occasionally during the summer, most plants can be put outside in the rain for a little while to be washed, because dust often accumulates on leaves and flowers.

All potted plants need occasional feeding with a liquid plant food, which can be bought from any gardening shop. Most plants do not like a room which is too hot and dry, neither do they like being in pro-longed sunshine. Do not leave plants between the drawn curtains and cold window glass on a frosty night.

If you should go away on holiday, and there is no-one who can water your pot plants, you can keep them moist by placing them in polythene bags, pot first, and tying the bags at the top. A polythene bag can also protect plants from draughts and cold in the winter in an unheated room. They will then need less water.